Telekinesis for Beginners: The Ultimate Guide to Moving Objects and Unleashing the Full Potential of Your Mind

Disclaimer and Terms of Use: Effort has been made to ensure that the information in this book is accurate and complete, however, the author and the publisher do not warrant the accuracy of the information, text and graphics contained within the book due to the rapidly changing nature of science, research, known and unknown facts and internet. The Author and the publisher do not hold any responsibility for errors, omissions or contrary interpretation of the subject matter herein. This book is presented solely for motivational and informational purposes only.

Table of Contents

Introduction

There are many people who would wish to have telekinesis abilities if they believed they existed. The problem is that we have been brought up to believe that these powers do not exist when they do. Another great news is that anyone can learn how to perform telekinesis. When you think about it actually, you already have those abilities inside you and all you have to do is make them active which can be achieved by putting in effort and practice. This book is meant to help you learn how to activate these abilities and apply them in your everyday life.

You might have watched movies where people seem to have the ability to toss cars around as if they are toys or lift some buildings. I hate to burst your bubble but this is not what we are talking about here. Telekinesis can help you move some small objects occasionally. There are few people who can learn to perform telekinesis on demand and you may be sitting on your abilities. For most people, these kinds of abilities appear in spurts. This is why some people do not believe it is real.

In telekinesis, your physical strength does not apply and all you need is your mental strength. This means that even people with disabilities are able to learn how to perform telekinesis just like everyone else. In fact, physically handicapped people are able to do this better because they have a higher level of concentration. The knowledge of telekinesis is starting to dawn on many people worldwide.

Chapter 1: Understanding the science of Telekinesis

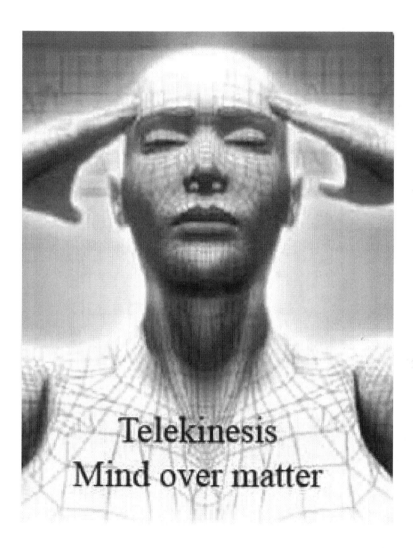

Have you ever found yourself in a situation where you are wishing the traffic lights would magically turn green so you can continue your journey or stared wishfully at a slot machine trying to create a match? Research shows that may be you should continue trying because you are able to do that through telekinesis. Telekinesis is all about being able to control the movements of objects by the power of your mind. This works by projecting a part of your conscious mind to the particular object you are looking to move.

What normally happens is that you concentrate on the object and make it part of yourself after which you will be able to move it. This is possible because at this point you consider yourself the third hand giving you the power to move.

Understanding telekinesis and the science behind it can help to increase your chances of succeeding at performing it.

1. **Understanding how important and possible telekinesis is**

Energy is simply the capacity to do work and out bodies are full of energy and this is what helps us to move, breathe and even work. This energy is obtained from the food we eat and is referred to as chemical energy. It is only about 40% of this energy that goes towards mechanical work. The process of cellular respiration releases potential chemical energy which is later turned in to kinetic energy when in the muscles. With regard to telekinesis, one uses the chemical body that is stored inside the body instead of using the potential chemical energy.

Although this chemical energy cannot be seen at least with the naked eye, it actually exists.

The initial law regarding thermodynamics states that it is not possible to create or destroy energy but it is able to be changed or transferred from a different form to another. The energy existing in any system is constant and this refers to the surroundings too. Contrary to popular belief, telekinesis is not magic. It is all about transferring energy from one's body which is the surroundings in this case to an object that regarded as the system because it is outside of the object.

2. **Recognize the energy flowing through your body**

Telekinesis exists with the mentality that you and the object you are trying to manipulate are one. This is why you need to feel this during the time you get the connection as it flows through your body. You can try out two exercises to test that.

Try stretching your arms in front of you and flex every muscle you have. You can do this for about 10 seconds and you can do this for your fist too. After the 10 seconds, relax your arm completely and try to get the feeling of heat that passes through it. You may experience something similar to an electrical sensation or the heat may pulse. What you feel after your muscle contracting is the energy we are referring to. Your aim therefore is to be able to control this energy without any kind of trigger such as the one required to move your muscles. When you have gotten to the point where you are able to do this then the next thing is learning to sustain the energy.

Another exercise you can try is looking for a suitably cold area where you can completely relax your body. You can choose to sit or lie in such a way that the hair on your body does not stand up. This exercise will require you to practice controlling the energy you will feel naturally trying to offer you heat in order to prevent you from freezing. When you gain control of this, you will be good at controlling the extra energy that goes into useless things. With time, you will know how to send transfer this energy from one part of your body to another for example your hand or chest whenever necessary.

3. Be specific on your way of manipulating the system

Since you will be manipulating the system, it is important to be specific about how you would like to do this. This is with regards to whether you are thinking of pushing, pulling or spinning it. It is easy to pull the system due to the fact that you will be having knowledge of the direction of energy. However, levitation is very hard because it requires minimizing the inertia the systems contain to be able to make it very light to enable the reaction of the system's electromagnetism and its surroundings.

When you want to alter the form of the system then you need to alter all the kinetic energy available in the system and this is what is commonly referred to as heat. The volume of the heat energy required to alter the system is counted in terms of calories which is equivalent to 4.184 joules. This is why it may be a bit difficult for your mind to alter the form of an object although it is possible.

4. Direct the energy towards their system

When you have the energy, you need to direct it to their system and how you do this is up to you. This is due to the fact that there are different methods that work for various people. Human beings think differently and since telekinesis is all about using the mind to manipulate objects then you need to find out the method that works for you. Before you get to this point, it is important to feel the system and try to figure out its weight, determine the amount of energy needed to physically move it. After doing that, try to see if you can match that same level of energy with the one you feel inside the body but when you are not physically touching the object.

What you have to keep in mind is that this process requires a continuous flow of energy. The minute you start the process of altering a system, don't stop. Focus your energy on it or else it will resume the primary state it was in according to Newton's first law which implies that something stays at rest until a force acts on it and that force is you.

When practicing telekinesis, you should know that if you focus for long durations then your system can be very exhausting which may lead to mild headaches once in a while. Although these headaches are not serious, they indicate that you should have some rest.

Throughout history, the person who had the strongest recorded telekinetic talent was Nina Kulagina who was a Russian housewife. However, even this strong woman was just able to make objects to roll and shift but not fully levitate. Through telekinesis, you can be able to manipulate objects in great deal of ways but this doesn't mean that you will be able to do a lot of impossible things whispered about telekinesis because some of them are merely illusions.

Chapter 2: Preparing to perform Telekinesis

Telekinesis has been under skepticism for years. Most of the times, people do not think about it due to the fact that they haven't experienced them. The fact that there hasn't been any science to back it up doesn't mean it isn't possible. As long as you have an open mind, you can try it. Learning telekinesis requires preparation because it is not something you just do at once.

1. **Practice your visualization skills**

Visualization is one of the most important exercises required in learning telekinesis whether it is about yourself or the objects around you. The exercises you are required to carry out cannot give you results if you don't back them up with skills which is where visualizing comes in. It works in the same way as meditation in the sense that you first see the desired outcome in your mind and then wish them to actually happen and work at it.

When you are ready to get into visualizing, you should start with small objects. Concentrate on every small detail and this may require feeling, smelling, getting the color and even taste of these objects until you get to the point where you are able to see the entire scene in your mind.

2. Meditate

Anyone who has knowledge of telekinesis knows that meditation is core in developing your superhuman skills. Your brain needs to be 100% clear in order for you to be able to channel the energy needed to control the objects around you. You should not have any other thoughts that could disrupt and distract you in order to have enough energy to channel in to controlling those objects you want. The fastest way of developing this skill is through meditation. Many people think that listening to music during meditation helps them to concentrate yet this is the opposite.

We normally live very busy lives that what you can do to be admired is juggle between lots of things at the same time. Meditation is a great way of escaping from all this hustle and bustle related to this kind of life. This is when your mental process comes into play.

3. Open you mind

Practice telekinesis works like hypnosis in the sense that you will not achieve the results you want when you have a closed mind. What you think is what will happen and so if you want to be able to do it then you might believe that. What you need is to ignore what people say and give it all you've got. When you don't believe then you should be sure that nothing will happen. However, if you believe then it's not a guarantee but there is a possibility it will happen. Learning telekinesis does not have leave room for doubts.

4. Be patient

Patience is paramount when learning telekinesis. When you look at the history of telekinesis, it took people years of practice to perfect the art. You cannot be sure of the moment when you will achieve that magical mixture of energy and so what you have to do is keep on practicing. This is not like losing weight where you witness the results gradually. Here, you have to keep on practicing until one day something happens since you don't know when that will be.

5. Relax

Relaxing is not usually an issue if you are good at meditating because you will have known how to channel the energy you require for telekinesis. Imagine a scenario where you are attempting to channel your energy but you are thinking about your job, relationship or any other thing. It will not be possible so the best thing to do is to relax. Just let yourself be in the moment and don't let your brain go away.

One great way of getting rid of the stresses we face in our everyday life is by doing yoga. Apart from yoga and meditation, you can try exercise in general. It is important to set aside some time for yourself every day to be able to relax. You don't have to take lots of time for this, about 15-20 minutes is enough and you will notice that your day will be better.

When you are performing telekinesis, you need to stop the trail of thought that the object you are trying to control is different from you. The whole idea is that both of you should be having the same energy. If you believe that the spoon you are trying to manipulate is a natural part of you then you can be able to move it.

Chapter 3: Learning how to perform Telekinesis

One of the most questions that people who have learnt about telekinesis ask is how they can be able to perform it. This doesn't mean that it is easy. In addition to that, you shouldn't think that there is a specific procedure that should be followed because the case of one-shoe-fits all doesn't apply here. There isn't a pattern style that works for everyone. People are different and the level of effort that you require for it relies on how your mind, body and soul react to the training. Most people need lots of effort for this to happen which may be the reason why most of them do not succeed.

One thing you have to know is that the fact that you reached a perfect combination one day is not a guarantee that it will be possible to get to that exact combination on the next day. The most important thing is to never get discouraged and keep on going to achieve the final results you want. When it comes to telekinesis, practice makes perfect. By following this guide, you can be able to successfully perform telekinesis.

1. Concentrate only on a small object

When you want to move the objects around you, you should channel your natural energy to doing that and this requires a high level of concentration. The easiest way of doing is by beginning with lightweight objects and examples include a small pencil or match. The easiest objects to manipulate are the ones with molecules that are far apart. When you have perfected this then you can move on to bigger objects.

You can try practicing these sessions about twice a day. An hour of this is enough in a day. Since you will have learnt about visualizing, you can try imagining the object moving. It is important to be specific about where you want the object to move whether it is to the right, left, if you want it to roll or whether you want the object to move.

2. Make psi balls

These are balls containing energy that you can be able to feel, manipulate and even use it to perform complicated tasks with time. You can start by holding your hands as if you are cupping a ball. Think of how big the ball is, whether it is radiating, and its color. After this image is concrete, you can make it move around before mopping the shape and size.

When you have perfected this art, you can move on to transferring this energy into other objects. Imagine how a baseball can knock a vase over and concentrate on your psi ball hitting objects that are real and it can happen.

3. **Do flamework**

Apart from dealing with small objects, you should try working with fire. Try lighting a candle and watch while it glows. After this, you need to clear your mind and fill it instead with the flame. Look at the flame as it flickers and use your energy to move it. You can practice moving it to the right, left, making it grow bigger or dimmer and basically get it to do anything that you want with your mind. You can even make it dance. Practicing with flames is recommended at first because they are easier to manipulate due to the fact that they are not weighty objects but balls of energy and so they won't put up much of a fight. This exercise is convenient especially when you are tired and are looking for an exercise to help you get started on telekinesis.

4. Switch up exercises

The fact that you will be doing telekinesis exercises for about an hour a day require you to switch up the exercises you do in order to avoid monotony and boredom since it is a long duration. The best way of identifying the methods that will work best for you and those that won't is by trying them out.

One technique you can try out is bending a spoon. Don't use your best china spoon to do this. Just take any spoon that you can do without and hold it horizontally in front of you with both of your hands. When doing this, ensure the handle is pointing up. Get your focus on the psi ball and imagine it getting hotter or brighter. Take the ball and move it through your arms and let it go to your fingers. At the end, your fingers should be able to bend the spoon as easily as butter. The best time to do this is when you feel like the psi ball has achieved its hottest point.

When trying this out, you can opt for an object that rolls. The best way to begin is by a light stroke and let your concentration be on the object zooming across the table. As days go by, lessen your poke but still put focus on maintaining the push. You can try working with a compass too. There are people who find it easier to work with it due to the fact that it is free floating. This is something you can concentrate on whether you have your eyes open or closed. When your eyes are closed then you need to wave your hand over it pointing in the direction that you want it to go. It is obvious that you require someone to monitor the ball in case you choose to do it with your eyes closed. Alternatively, you can use a camera to monitor it.

5. Try astral projection

This simply refers to out-of-body-experiences and it is a situation where your soul departs from your body and goes on astral plane. For you to do this, you need to be in a very deep state of hypnosis. When your body enters the state of "vibration," your soul moves from your body and enters the world around you.

Although it may sound easy, this is quite a difficult thing to do. It is advisable to start small in order to avoid frustrations. You can try moving your arm or leg and get to experience the out-of-limb-experience. After that, you will be able to move to your entire self and you can wander around to the different rooms and then into the atmosphere. This thought might be very scary but don't give in to the fear, just relax and you will be able to get back to your body.

6. Stop when you get tired

These exercises can tire you out especially if you don't have enough rest and so whenever you feel like you are exhausted either mentally or physically, get enough rest and make sure you only continue when the fatigue has worn off and you are back to normal. You will be able to get better results when you feel refreshed. The best way to know if you are up for the exercises is to listen to what your body and mind tells you.

Chapter 4: Telekinesis Exercises you can try out

Do you ever think about how powerful your mind is? Well, when you get the right motivation, effort and guidance, you can be able to do things you didn't even know were possible. You have the power to make objects move from one location to another without necessarily touching them physically. Our minds are full of energy which is controllable and this is the power that telekinesis applies. When you are beginning, you need to know how to tap into your concentration powers and you can only go on getting started on telekinesis after you have mastered it. We have talked about how important concentration is in the previous chapters but you can learn the actual techniques of achieving this.

1. Technique for developing concentration powers

When you are just training yourself to concentrate, you can begin by sitting in a dark room and have nothing but a candle for company. The candle should stay at a corner of the room you are in order to avoid getting the flame affected by things such as the wind or even your own breath. Your focus should be on the candle's flame and clear your mind of everything else from thoughts to sounds. When you are sure that nothing can distract you can focus on your breathing and try to see if you can hear your own heartbeat. When you hear this then you can be sure that you are focused enough to begin. The next step is observing the candle's flame and trying to feel the energy flowing out of that flame.

Another technique you can apply is using a sheet of paper. This paper should be plain and should have a single black dot. You can try focusing on that dot every day for about 15 minutes or more. This will help to greatly improve your concentration power.

2. Exercises for moving objects

When you have mastered your concentration technique and are ready to start moving objects then you can engage in the exercises that can help you accomplish this. What you have to know at this stage is that you need to exercise your mind on a daily basis. This requires moving things and making tem change the way you desire.

• Moving the pendulum

Find a pendulum or make one at home by the help of a cork that is hung by a string. Get this pendulum in a place that is not near the windows and doors and this can be in a corner of a given room. Put all your energy on the pendulum using your power of concentration and try picturing it moving. Visualization falls under the easiest methods in terms of setting the pendulum in motion. Alternatively, you can use the movement of your eyes to achieve the same results. The latter method requires more effort though that doesn't mean it isn't worth a try. When you are beginning, it is better to start with lighter objects due to the fact that they are easier to move. Since this activity requires lots of mental strength, it is normal to feel worn out but ensure you rest for a while before resuming when feel tired.

- **Floating the flower**

This requires you to fill a bowl with water and then place a toothpick or flower so they can float on water. Choose a steady place to put the bowl of water and make sure there aren't any vibrations that can interfere with it.

You can begin by carrying out some exercises on concentrating as you wait for the water to become still. When this happens, the flower or the object you picked will be resting at one corner of the bowl. Put your concentration on the toothpick or flower for quite some time before channeling your energy to the task of causing ripples inside the water. Don't take your focus away from the toothpick or flower and move the one you are using around the bowl. Therefore, it should be swirling around the bowl. When you succeed at this, you can try to return things back to normal by making the water still they way it was initially. A maximum duration of fifteen minutes is recommended for this exercise.

3. Exercises for changing an object's shape

The better you get at practicing telekinesis then you can move away from the small objects to advanced exercises and this can be trying to change an object's shape. The first exercise you can start with involves rolling the edges of paper all by the help of your mind. When you get good at this then you can move on to bending things after which breaking things follow. Although focusing on a flame can enhance your concentration power, an advanced step requires you to actually bend the flame to the direction of your choice. When you succeed at this, then you can try this technique on a spoon. The steps you require at this stage involve focusing, becoming one with the object, requesting to change that object and then using all the stored energy you have to actually bend the cutlery or various objects you desire. This activity is more intense than the previous ones so the importance of good rest cannot be overemphasized. When you feel tired, the best thing to do is rest.

4. Exercises for holding objects in mid air

When you have passed all the other steps then the last step of telekinesis is training to hold objects in mid air. When you are beginning this stage, it is advisable to begin with small objects and when you have perfected the then you can try heavier objects such as chairs. The first step here is concentrating on your palms and rubbing them in order to move energy into them. The motions of your hands will thereafter guide you in your attempt to lift things such as stationary, coins, containers and so on. It is important to use your eyes to control the objects in order to prevent them from falling to the ground. This means that there is absolutely no room for distraction even just for a minute. It is easier to channel energy in to smaller items and hold them in mid air.

Telekinesis is not something that you can effectively master in a single day. That is why there are different stages and these guide you in the journey of learning to move objects using your mind. Therefore lots of dedication, practice and perseverance can go a long way towards increasing your chances of succeeding. However, there are four golden rules that guide you if you apply them with regards to learning to perform telekinesis.

The first one is that all objects contain energy. It is possible to use the human mind to control this energy existing in objects. When there is permeation of two powers, the result is a stronger power and lastly, the entire process carried out to practice telekinesis is incomplete if there is no communication.

Chapter 5: Common mistakes to avoid when learning Telekinesis

Learning telekinesis is a gradual process that takes time and patience to perfect. For some people this may be days while for others it may be months. In the process of learning telekinesis, there are some mistakes you might end up making along the way and knowing some of the common ones that have been made by other people can help you avoid them.

1. Self- reflection

Many people normally disregard the part about doing things yourself which is part of the training for telekinesis and this is especially among beginners. There hasn't been any sound formula to explain how telekinesis works and this is why many people are left to explore and discover their personal features. Research about telekinesis is important in guiding you on how to go about the process itself but you also need self-reflection to actually help you break through. What this means is that you will know all that you need to about telekinesis but the rest of it with regard to whether or not it will work out depends on you. This is why you need moments of self-reflection which will help you to understand yourself more. You will be able to decide on what you are imagining inside and know the reason for it. The results will be knowing yourself more and greatly increasing your chances of succeeding at telekinesis. This is due to the fact that knowing yourself more often comes with feelings of self-worth which is important in life in general and also in being successful at telekinesis.

Skipping this part therefore is a mistake you should avoid when you decide to try out telekinesis. Most people are more interested in getting to the part where they are able to move objects yet good things take time to accomplish and require following the necessary steps. Although this appeal is quite strong and natural, be willing to follow the right procedure to increase your results of achieving success.

2. Resonance

Resonance refers to the moments when there are several related vibrations that bond to create a greater push with more emphasis on the metaphysical or metaphorical aspect. After the doing it yourself step that requires self-reflection, you will have a better understanding of yourself and you feel much closer to yourself. This enables you to think and accept some things that the society doesn't even believe in. This will put you a step ahead of someone who wants to practice telekinesis but hasn't come to this point of believing in it.

Resonance will help in the sense that the more you believe in something, the more you feel it, sing it from within and you will generally have a positive attitude about it. This will enable you to align the beliefs that will encourage you to move on.

If you are performing telekinesis and you find something appearing odd then you should avoid it and it doesn't matter if it has been recommended by experts. It is okay to have your own beliefs. We have already stated that there hasn't been a clear path defined for conducting telekinesis and so who knows? Your way might be right or you might have discovered something. Therefore, if something feels right for you, explore it.

3. Letting go

What you have to know about letting go is that it is an important part of telekinesis. Generally, people are usually shunned when they try to exceed their own limitations and we are only supposed to conform to society's standards. We are normally told of our limitations from the time we are young and some of them are eve passed down to us from our parents, guardians and the people we look up to. This makes it easy for us to be satisfied with not reaching our full potential. This is something that can hinder you from succeeding at telekinesis because it requires a high level of belief. One way of removing these self doubts that you may be having is through self-reflection which we have mentioned. You can try to change every thought you have towards the positive. Of course, you will find yourself having negative thoughts once in a while but if you train yourself to turn them around to the positive ones then you will notice a change after some time.

You can practice letting go whenever you experience negative thoughts. Normally, your first instincts will be to try and fight them and this will not put you in that calm frame of mind required for telekinesis. Practice taking deep breaths and telling yourself that everything will be okay and let your mind wander to something else. In case it is difficult to stop thinking about the particular negative thing on your mind, you can still breathe deeply before becoming aware of yourself because your mind might be trying to deal with that particular thought in real time.

Always remember that fear, doubt or negativity comes about when you are scared of your own inability which means that you have what it takes to perform telekinesis. Sometimes, you will discover that you feared for no good reason. Tell yourself you are strong and leg to. With time, things will begin to flow naturally for you.

4. Proper focus

You require proper focus for you to develop telekinesis even though it is important in various areas of your life. Most people often focus by straining or putting in lots of efforts. When they put their minds on something, they often try including muscle power in it. This is especially the case with telekinesis since the tasks that are supposed to be performed require force in ordinary circumstances but the rules change and mental focus is needed here. When things don't go our way, it is human nature to put in more force and it is easy for this to create a vicious cycle leading to lots of stress and frustrations which doesn't help with the telekinesis exercises.

The best way of achieving focus is by being in a relaxed state. Just sit somewhere, relax and open your mind. There will be creation of free space within you and you will have room to breathe. This is the right time for taking your object and trying to move or manipulate it the way you want. Don't give it much thought, instead let yourself feel the experience. The next thing is you will start to sense the object and will feel like you have a connection to it. It is not even important t try and find out what this connection is because you might take your focus from the main issue.

When you have this connection, try and move the object. You can imagine there is a force beside the object gently touching it or it may be an innate energy that is beginning to move. Try to make this imagination as realistic as possible. This is a very important point because it is normally the point where most people question how legitimate what they are doing is or try to rationalize it and this may mess up the entire procedure. Don't be too hard on yourself because you will need to practice this for some time before you become good at it. When you are practiced this, the object will be more likely to start moving. However, do not hold on to this expectation so much because you might get disappointed since results are not guaranteed and other times it may take time.

Final thoughts

Different people have various things to say about telekinesis with regards to whether it is real or not. There are people who can attest to the fact that it does actually exist and they have either been able to perform it or have seen others do it. However, this is something that you can find out on your own. What you have to know is that results are not guaranteed and while it may be easy for some people, it might take much more effort for others.

This book is important for you if you have decided to give telekinesis a try. It is important not to ignore the preparations required for this to happen. When you apply the tips highlighted here and actually try out the various exercises shown, you greatly increase your chances of succeeding at telekinesis.

Before you begin this journey, you have to be prepared for the fact that it is not easy and it requires putting in a lot of work, dedication and perseverance. If there is even a tiny chance that you can use the power of your mind to manipulate objects around you then why shouldn't you take it? This is a chance to explore your full potential and who knows? You might be one of the few who have exceptional abilities of doing this. If this is something you would like to try out then, good luck. If not then you might share this information with those around because you might never know who it might interest. All the best!

Yours Sincerely,

David.

84997344R00027

Made in the USA
San Bernardino, CA
14 August 2018